A Book of Chrissyisms

The Only Way to Find Art is to Lose Touch with Reality

by

Christina Strigas

A Book of Chrissyisms

The Only Way to Find Art is to Lose Touch with Reality

by Christina Strigas

Books by Christina Strigas

Poetry

Love & Vodka
In Your Own Flood
Your Ink on My Soul

Novels

The Wanting
Crush: A Paranormal Romance Novel
Althia's Calling
Althia's Journey
Althia's Awakening

Copyright © 2018 by Christina Strigas

First edition, 2018

All rights reserved, including the right to reproduce this book or portions thereof in any form whatsoever.

The use of any part of this publication, reproduced, transmitted in any form or by any means electronic, mechanical, photocopying, recording or otherwise, or stored in retrieval system without the prior written consent of the publisher, or in the case of photocopying or other reprographic copying, license from the Canadian Copyright Licensing Agency is an infringement of the copyright law.

Library and Archives Canada Cataloguing in Publication Data is available upon request.

ISBN: 9780995186583

Book and Cover design by Christina Strigas

Book edited and formatted by Deborah A. Bowman, CEO, Clasid Consultants Publishing, bowmaneditor@outlook.com

Contact author christinastrigasauthor@gmail.com for written permission to reproduce any parts of this book.

"What is reality?
I am a plaster doll; I 'pose."

- Anne Sexton from "Self in 1958"

Dear Reader,

I don't try to make people laugh or cry. I know the way I think is different. I know the way I feel everything is not the same as everyone else. I can pretty much cry at a commercial and feel sick to my stomach over shootings. I have a big world in my head. My trees are purple; my sky is sometimes grey, sometimes a rainbow. You might think I'm smiling, but really, I'm not.

I say dumb, smart, wise, silly, and brilliant things every day. No one is following me with a pen.

I suppose it's time to share my thoughts and make people feel uncomfortable.

I don't want to write a best seller. I gave up on that dream as soon as I made it.

I want to share my *meraki,* my soul, with you. My true identity changes daily. One day, I'm full of life; the next day, I'm empty. My journal is null and void; my journal is full. I am typing into midnight or not as sad as I think I am.

I think this book will be good for people who don't go for walks. I think this book is good for the people who drive too much. Perhaps you'll like my poems or my thoughts or my weird comments. I have a wise mouth, and I know I'm brave with words.

Some people are courageous with actions.

I have words.

They are my armour.

My saviour.

I hope you can learn something.

After all, I am a teacher.

Please feel free to tell me anything. I try to give more than I receive.

I Love You,

Chrissy

"I don't trust Google."

I think Google is trying to control me. Once, I used to look inside a World Book Encyclopaedia, and now I find that Google tells me what to think and how to find the wrong answer. I spent way too much time researching "how to make a multi-boxed book set" than is necessary. It was a waste of time and energy. I could have been reading my book, but I clicked on nonsense and read more nonsense, got off topic, and therein lies my wasted time and energy. Hence, I don't believe Google has my best interests when I search for a word.

The World Book Encyclopaedia did. I searched for a word or a country or a bird, and there was one answer. I believed in the Encyclopaedia. Now, you're not supposed to trust Wikipedia anymore. Fill your brain with doubt. Fill your thoughts with innocence. It is complicated research to find one word that equals one million clicks and no right answer. It's up to you to decide.

I want to go back to the library and find the books that tell me the truth.

Do you have a quarter?

When I was young, I had quarters in my pockets for a phone call. Now I have a debit card for everything. If I misplace my debit card, I can go to the bank and get a new one. If I lose my money, there is no getting it back. I prefer to live dangerously and have cash on me. I prefer to pay with bills and confuse the young cashiers who can't add any more. I prefer to not have air miles and fly for free because I'm poor anyway. If all we do is compare purses, then I'll daydream about being at the BookCon. It costs $1,650 dollars to get a press kit and sell your books there. It costs $1,549 for that purse. I don't even have to think of the choice I would make. I saw a lot of the Instagram poets I first started out within 2015 there. It made me sad to think of all the ways I could have sold my soul to be there too, smiling and taking selfies. It made me proud to think of all the ways I did not sell my soul to sell more books.

I keep quarters in my pockets to remind me of all the times I stopped my car to call my mother and tell her I was safe.

I'm an adult now; I use my cell phone. Everyone knows where I am at all moments of the day. I wish I could disappear for a few hours, so I could put my phone on airplane mode.

When someone does not own a phone, we stare in awe because we can't Airdrop a photo, but really, we are envious of that person because they still use their quarters.

Expectations will ruin your life

Most people have these unrealistic expectations of their loved ones when they know that they have limitations. I can't expect my husband to take out the trash when he never does. I can't be disappointed in my book sales when I don't promote myself like I need to. I can't expect my friends to read my mind when I run out of restaurants upset.

I hate to feel so much. At the same time, I don't know what it's like to feel nothing at all. Most people can't see the cracks in the sidewalk because they are staring at their phones. I read a whole book on a plane and had time to drink. I feel that expectations should be kicked away as far away from reality as possible. Paths have a way of turning into gravel and detour signs are more prevalent now more than ever.

I am working on a book, a journal, a new life.

Chapters don't need headings all the time.

Life needs to be unpredictable or you'll be trapped in boredom.

"I'm in and out."

Scene 1

In Vancouver waiting in line to go to a breakfast joint.

"Would you come back?" my friend asks me.

"From where?" I ask.

She laughs, "Here, what do you think I'm talking about?"

"Oh…" The reality hit me. I was thinking of fantasy land. I was dreaming awake. "No, I want to stay in my fantasy. I like it better than reality."

Scene 2

"Pardon me?"

"You're not listening to me."

"'I'm in and out," I say.

"Of what?"

"Reality."

Giving as a way of life

I made the Greek coffee at ten years old, and I am still making the coffee.

I am still giving.

One day perhaps I will get back.

I can't think that way.

I will cry too much.

When someone brings me a coffee or makes me a meal, it is the most precious gift to me.

I don't care about designer shoes or purses, although they are lovely.

I would rather someone bring me their honesty in a cup of latte.

My daughter made this vegan dish with cashew and milk and I was surprised because someone else besides me made a meal. I was so excited to receive this free gift that she did not even realize she gave me. I ate it with so much love. It filled my stomach with a fullness no other meal has before.

These are the most precious moments.

Giving and receiving without acknowledging it or throwing it in anyone's face.

In its purest form. In silence.

For a meal made from love as I sit in a café writing about it and crying.

The more you do for people, the less you matter

Everyone takes advantage of a soft person. You may be called "enabler" because you listen and don't judge or form an instant opinion. You may be the only person making the coffee at your house, but that's your pleasure. It's when your family and friends stop noticing and appreciating you that you feel like you can instantly turn into the actual doormat and understand expressions.

It is hard to stop doing when all you know how to do is the act of doing. Go. Go. Go. Do. Do. Do.

Make the coffee, make the breakfast, grocery shop, make the menu, walk the dog, clean the house, wash the clothes, make more lists, take out the garbage, go get the dry cleaners, pick up the kids, drive the kids, answer the emails, plan the vacation, make sure the cupboards are properly stored with everything you will need. Everything is in its place because of you. No one understands or cares how hard that is to do on a daily basis. You seem to disappear into the kitchen. Lose track of time and place because you cook, do the dishes, and mop the floor alone again.

Be brave and do less. You'll see you matter more when the world tilts its axis. Disappear for a few days. You'll see how life goes on without you.

And then you'll start to matter to yourself again.

So much pressure to be someone else; choose yourself and be innovative

The worst thing you can do to yourself is comparing and contrasting your life with others. Someone checked in at a restaurant on Facebook; another person is at the gym. Someone else is celebrating, toasting, always smiling.

Stop wanting someone else's life; we all know the saying, "The grass is never greener on the other side." There's a reason for that saying…stop looking so hard at others and find what makes you want to change the world for a better place. One act and you have done something. Anything but stare at a phone and want the fantasy.

The only **person** you need to compare yourself with is **You.**

update your status
change your profile pic
take a picture of your salad
how about putting the phone away?
how about having a real conversation about
how beautiful you are today?
how about you do nothing
but share real-time
with loved ones.

Social media can hurt you more than you can imagine

I cried when Christy died…she was my sweet friend from Twitter. Although I had never met her or talked to her on the phone, she always sent me kind messages and warm wishes for years.

Other people on social media claim to be your friend and plagiarize you or catfish you. You can mute and block strangers. You can become close friends, enemies.

It's a war zone.

It's torture explaining your empathy to unsympathetic people

It's hard to explain why I'm crying all the time. I don't even want to anymore. It's the way I am. I feel too much. I sense a storm and lock down my windows. I hate explaining why…specifically to people who never cry at movies. I mostly keep silent because there is so much going on in my mind.

It's exhausting being a Woman.

Cook
Wash
Fold
Clean up
Make the bed
Shop
Make the lists
Call the doctors
Buy clothes
Call the teachers
Plan the summer
Do homework
Drive
Organize
Watch games
Prepare snacks
Prepare lunches
Bathe
sleep

Keep evolving, life is boring being the **same person**

I was a cleaning lady
I worked at a boutique
I taught adults
inside restaurants, during breaks
I taught businesspeople
toddlers
pre-schoolers
high school students
adults
elementary students
I was a barmaid
I was a daughter
I was a girlfriend
I was a lover
a wife
a mother
a writer
a poet
I am never the same for long.
A chameleon.

Judge less, ignore more

stop gossiping
about what he said
what she said
what he did
what she did
what they do
what we do
stop listening to others versions of others
creating labels in your heads about others
making yourself feel better
by judging
look inwards
ignore those people who gossip
say, "let's talk about you."
not them.
It's okay to be yourself
to leave the politeness for once
to turn your back when you don't want to talk
to say hello when you need
to trust in people.
"Ignorance is Bliss,"
Socrates said.
He was right.

Ignoring people is my own self-healing

I can choose to talk to someone who only talks about themselves and their own accomplishments or I can get up and choose to talk to the person that everyone hates in the room.

I did that once.

It was quite astonishing to realize that she was reserved, quiet, and introspective. She was smart, had a Ph.D., and kept to herself.

She was soothing to talk to, a great listener, and had more to say than everyone combined in that room.

You think you know me, but you don't.

Everyone is an expert on you.
Oh, you are so funny
(you did not see me balling my eyes out this morning over my coffee).
Oh, you are a best-selling poet
(you do not know how many rejections I have and how many times I wish I weren't).
Oh, you are a teacher
(you do not know how I wish to write all day and night and not have a day job).
Oh, you have two kids
(actually, I had four pregnancies).
Shall I go on?
You get the picture now.
Two faces or three or four.
It depends on the day or night.

Stop explaining yourself and listen to the silence

The main reason you need a dog is that it forces you to take a walk.

It forces you to listen to nature in the early morning or late in the evening.

Every day is different too. Every sunset.

You can witness it by walking with your dog.

It's the perfect excuse to leave the house and listen to the silence.

When people ask you questions, you can pretend you didn't hear them. That works too. Or change the subject. You don't owe anyone an explanation. You do owe yourself a quiet walk with your dog.
I think, Spunky, my dog, has saved my life.

Being

extraordinary is

hard to **hide.**

You can tell when someone

loves your madness

cares about how you care about the moon

loves you for your humor

more than your normal

sees how you sing with no voice

talks you through trauma, stress

notices your new hairstyle

knows when you cried

grasps your aura

from the moment you first met

and rocks you to sleep

at any age.

People suffer daily with a smile.

Be timeless

Inspired by "Timeless" by The Airborne Toxic Event.

I was in Boston with my girlfriends and fell upon one of my favorite band's live show.

This song is an ocean of unanswered questions.

Do something that is timeless.

Disappear into yourself and find out what you want to do with your life. It's never too late to begin fresh. You can't do the same thing for thirty years, work in the same company, live in the same house. It's time to change and be timeless. Learn how to be a vampire without altering your mortality.

New chapters make you timeless. Live forever by changing.

Life is not as short as you think. Live in a moment and it lasts longer.

Everyone says life is short. In essence, if you live in the moment, it lasts longer. If you put your phone away, you have better conversations—you are less distracted; you focus on your loved ones; you feel connected.

Take time to do nothing. Sit and look out into your backyard: the sky, the trees, your garden; listen to the birds. If you are in the city, put some flowerpots on your balcony, get fake green grass, walk barefoot.

Drink your morning coffee on the balcony, watch people walk by, wave good morning, talk to your neighbor. Ask them how they are feeling today. Lift your head up and stop staring at your phone—it makes you lose your concept of time and sucks you into a vortex of forgetfulness.

That dead feeling, but you're still breathing

When you feel like the world is crashing right before you, you can deal with it: the car won't start; the shoes won't fit; your waist is too thick; the painting does not match anymore; the school keeps calling; you're already ten minutes late—yet, there you are. You show up.
You say, "Good morning!" and start teaching your class.

I don't have a mental illness; I don't use my mental health as a crutch to sell my books or my humanity. I keep private about such matters. I'm not judging, I'm just saying. If I break down in my car while listening to a song, I'm not the first. You can't keep on being "proper" forever.

I wake up every day and it's a new day. I could be some kind of Greek Buddhist. It makes me breathe easier. Being forgetful is easier than remembering everything and holding grudges.

I know I'm still fighting, like that day when I drove to the hospital and the school called. I had to be at two places at the same time. It was hard to choose between my father and my daughter, but I kept on breathing.

Being brave can make you uncomfortable, but it's necessary.

When you have to stand up for your child or yourself or someone close to you, be brave. Speaking up is free. Keeping quiet is tragic. If you want something to be private, then please keep it to yourself; however, when you have to confront someone over how they treat you or when you have to fight for your kids' battles because they rely on you—don't stop. Keep fighting and telling your truth.

You can be uncomfortable by speaking up, but better than suffering inside.

The most necessary things are hard to do.

The people who make you feel like not talking are the ones you need to get away from

These people talk too much and have no idea how to listen or read your body language. They are so engrossed in their own lives or stories that you come secondary all the time.

The older I get, the more I realize how much I need to listen to my thoughts more than gossip and the history of someone's life over and over again.

If someone remembers to ask about your life after two hours into a monopolized conversation, then you know, this is not the type of friend you want in your life.

This actually happened to me. After listening to a narcissist go on and on about how great her life is, how perfect her new husband is, how phenomenal her children are, how she is finally happy, how horrible her ex-husband is, *how, how, how*…I kept getting up to leave her house.

After the tenth time, after two hours of talking, she asked, "So, what's new with you? How are the kids?" That was my cue to get the fuck out of that kitchen and never step back into her life again.

Don't waste your **words** on someone who doesn't know how **to listen.**

Love with all you got or get out of the way

Most of the time I see the good in people up until they prove me wrong. Then I cross the street and walk alone.

I give love, but at a certain point, I need to receive it too. What's your language of love?

The easiest way to know how to be loved is to find out how you love. Do a quiz. Figure out your language of love and simplify your life. Ask for what you need or get out of the way. You can't force people to love you.

There are other paths and other chances to take if the one you are on is blocked. We have love in our hearts to give to someone, not to keep it locked up and saddened.

Keep loving hard.

The only way to find yourself is to lose yourself

Sometimes, I want to live another life. Other times, I want to stay put. There is this constant urge to write, but life and social media get in the way.

Jan. 2, 2018

Disappearing into yourself and your thoughts is a must for anyone—not just artists. Take time to lose the concept of time and working around the clock; be a Buddhist for a day.

Be **true** to the **artist** in you and the **art** will be true to you.

Keep dreaming and living the life you dare to live

When we are young, parents tell us we can be anything we want to be—except it's not true. I realized this when my father kept pushing me to study Commerce instead of English Literature.

What are you going to do with that degree?

This was the theme of my life. I had to go on and do a teaching degree to make a living because telling people that all I wanted to do was write was unrealistic. I kept writing in private, and only when I turned 39 did I first publish a novel. Thus far, I have self-published all my three poetry books and published two novels with MuseItUp Publishing company.
There is no money to be made unless you are J.K Rowling. No one writes for fame; it's all about the need to get out the words.

Despite it all, I pursue writing because it's part of who I am. I make peanuts, but I don't care. I love to write, and I am so grateful that there are readers who like to read my books.

I studied English Literature and Poetry, and I can't see myself doing anything else in my life. To make actual money, I teach. Teaching is part of my blood as well. It does not feel like work.

Do what you love with a passion—that is priceless.

I have nothing to say and everything to write

When you are a writer, all the words pour out of you while writing.

I'd rather write than talk. I am not one for small talk, but I am trying; the first step was asking my neighbor her name after two years. She's really sweet too, and she has health issues.

I listen and take notes in my head. I can't come up with solutions to problems on the spot. My friend Tina is like bang, bang, bang; here you go! Solution! I'm still registering the problem, thinking about it.

I'm timing my sunsets with my walks with Spunky to have more to write.
Each sunset is different.

Being a writer is an oddity

"I love what you write."

"I never met a writer before."

"I follow you."

"I'm your fan."

"She writes poetry books." I smile, oddly.

"I don't read poetry."

"I don't read books."

I nod my head and don't know what to say to people who don't read. Let's talk about the weather.

"That's fine. It's a beautiful day." I hope she does not ask me what inspires me, and I hope I don't have to explain how weird I am.

"Yes, it's a fine day."
"Phew." But, they look at me strangely. Suddenly, I feel naked, fully dressed.

Make

reality

**better
than**

fantasy.

Being an artist can make you or break you.

I'm as fragile as a piece of paper and as tough as a hard book cover

Books are simply an extension of me. I can be delicate or tough.

Do you ever find yourself in a situation that defines you? Do you ever ask yourself how can I make it out of this? Most times, we are on our own. Who do I call? How do I do it without my parents? My husband? My wife? How can I go on? Somehow or other…we find the strength in us to be strong and to guard our vulnerabilities. I show my weakness, my emotions—I can't seem to hide them well. I have learned to protect my shell; life teaches you how to be like a book.

All we want is someone to love our flaws more than our strengths

Imagine how much love you would feel if all the things you hate about yourself, someone said how beautiful they were.

Imagine how all your faults would turn into jewels that someone loved because that is what makes you shine.

It's not how strong you are; it's how you fuck it up sometimes. It's someone telling you, *"It's going to be okay. You'll get through this…"*

Our flaws are what makes us different. Embrace it. Heck, I'm actually naming them as *Chrissyisms*. For people that know me, fucking up and misunderstanding things is a daily fault of my character. My kids call me *"Muzzer"*. Making up nicknames for yourself is fun, or better yet, ask your loved ones to do that. It makes you who you are.

I have come to embrace all the silly dumb things I say. I have come to embrace all the witty ways my mind works. It's a balance. That's where we must live. In the balance between.

Freedom is not answering questions

People want to know why this or why that: why did you do that; why did you not…

Who says you have to answer and defend yourself?

Who says you have to have all the answers?

I dislike when people put me on the spot. I hate to reply as to what or why or when I am doing something that is a private matter. Sometimes it's no one's business. You need not fall into the trap of explaining yourself.

Be free to get up and excuse yourself. Say you don't want to talk about that now. Whatever you want to say. I have found myself in situations in which I don't want to tell anyone anything. When I feel like opening up and telling someone something personal, I will do it. Maybe never. You don't owe anyone an answer or an explanation.

There is nothing wrong with keeping things to yourself. Some people are private. Your loved ones or friends or acquaintances who love you have to respect you and not make you feel inadequate or that there is something wrong with you for not sharing. When you are ready to answer, you will. Perhaps, you won't. That's fine too.

Make others Feel Extraordinary

Showing you care is a way to make others feel like you matter—this could come from a complete stranger or a loved one. My husband is great at this. He can make people feel so special by complimenting them and making their day. Whatever your age, whatever your sex, he has that ability to make others feel extraordinary. I envy that. I try my best to be that way by seeing the beauty and good of others. I usually do; it takes me a while to figure out someone is using me, and see their bad. My way of showing love is by doing things for others.
I do, do, do.
I keep doing until I am exhausted. I should talk more and compliment more; I'm not sure what is better, but I do know that making someone feel special is a gift.
We need to give more and take less.

I am
more comfortable
being misunderstood

People will judge you all the time
you connect
you disconnect
they are there to talk
or gossip
about your last post
your last trip
your last meal
your kids
your hair
eyes
face
makeup.
It's a non-stop bombardment
of nonsense
unimportant bullshit.
Stay focused on who you are
beneath all the misunderstandings —
it's who you really are — inside where
the camera can't reach
that matters most.
The stuff eyes can't see.
The truth behind the sky.

I have learned to cradle silence in public places.

There are moments
I want to speak up
But I sit there in silence
Swallowing my words
Thinking no one cares
What I have to say.
It's mostly because I'm shy
Intimidated
Thinking to myself
Disagreeing with the yes vote.
I'm not a hypocrite.
I merely
Learned to keep the silence
Inside.
I'm happier that way
Keeping all these opinions to myself
And only sharing them with a certain few
I trust.

Poetry makes me realize how mad I truly am

By mad,
I mean
crazy over the words,
classic poems
modern poems
the form + technique
alliteration
sounds rolling off my tongue
Shakespeare's sonnets
Anne Sexton's *Selected Poems*
Sylvia Plath's *Ariel*
100 Love Sonnets of *Pablo Neruda*
while others are watching game shows and laughing
I'm thinking
I could write a poem about this now.

Take a social media break over the summer

Go on vacation and get off the grid. Cuba is an ideal place to go— Cuba has no free Wi-Fi anywhere. You have to pay, and no one wants to pay for Wi-Fi. Take a trip to the ocean; text no one. White sandy beach and turquoise waters.

Bond with your family.

Forget social media for a while; nothing will happen to your accounts. You might lose a few followers, but your sanity, health, and well-being are worth losing followers. Also, the people that love your writing will always follow you. If you're a writer go off the grid and don't even write or read; just be alive!

Know the difference between a story- teller and a listener

Sometimes you talk to people who only hear themselves or relate to your words according to their own experiences. They are prone to not give you good advice, but instead, tell you about their life and try to find some comparison that does not help you at all. Try to understand that these types are talkers, not listeners. They don't know how to listen. It's not their fault. They are storytellers. Know who to talk to and who to listen to. Sometimes they could be the same person, count yourself lucky; but most times, they are not the same person.

Freedom is writing all the things you cannot say

You sit there in your own silence
surrounded by your friends
family, colleagues
but you're stuck in a stutter
you can't take the day off
you can't write now
but the words are on your fingertips
not on your tongue.

You sit there in your own silence
it comforts you
but watching your night turn its back
is not what you need.

You would rather write
and there is nothing wrong with that
absolutely nothing
wrong with you
except how your mind
tells you otherwise.

In the end, you keep going back to the beginning.

There is always that one person
who makes you feel
as if
you are the only one
whoever mattered to them.
You feel as if
something is missing
you start over
realize you're at the beginning
every time with the wrong ending.

Life continues,
the time has a way
of tricking you into situational
lies, but you know deep down
that your guts
are what you should be listening to
not your heart
not your mind
not your body.
Your guts have a whole story
waiting for you to catch on.

The trick is to go in and out of reality with no detection

In French, we say, "Tu es dans la lune." *You are on the moon* is the literal translation, but you get the gist. Being in and out of reality is tricky. One minute you're listening to someone the next minute your attention is completely gone and you are in your own mind daydreaming. Nodding your head ever so often works and agreeing with whatever you're not listening to or better yet getting up and leaving the conversation is what you truly want to do, but don't want to appear rude. This is a hard skill, but in order to survive, we must learn to perfect this.

What I could naturally do as a child, is block everyone completely off. If I am in a group of people and one person is talking to me, I cannot hear the other conversations around me. It amazes me when people are capable to jump from one conversation to another. When I'm talking to my friend Helen, and she does that, I get so confused. Like, how did she even hear what they were saying…she says she can listen to many conversations at the same time. Hell, I have a hard time with one!

I tend to daydream and go off in my own world…half the time I'm in and out. I guess I was born this way, but I have come to terms with it and although some people might find me "ditzy" for not "paying attention" in my own head, well…I'm writing a book. This is the hardest to perfect. I find this one tricky, but once you've perfected it, you will be my idol.

Love is not the silent
treatment

I hate when someone you love uses the silent treatment to make a point that is not the point anymore. Don't take away communication to send a message. That's passive-aggressive love, and I want none of that. It is a slow killer of love. Love needs communication and hugs, constant water, an abundance of internal growth. When you take away words, you kill the love.

There's a time for silence, and there's a time for love.

The one thing about my husband is he can't keep quiet. He always brings out my silence.

People think they know you just because they love you.

When people tell me what to do, I do the **opposite.**

Have an opinion and be free of labels

Labels tie you down
they don't define you
they want to own you
      make you slide into a name
          that is not the complete part of you
          but only a fraction of you.

Face it. You're on your own.

No matter how much help you get
You still have to do things alone
Muster the courage
To walk alone
It's glorious
To be that way
In your mind
You are brave
For being yourself
There is nothing wrong
With doing it this way.

Love is your secret weapon

I hate worrying, but it's part of loving

I want to know my loved ones are safe. If I look at my son's texts, most of them consist of the same line "Where are you?"
My daughter tells me exactly where she is; but I still text her constantly, nagging her. "I'm Greek, that's what we do. We drive our kids crazy!" I say.
It's a stressful world; there are drugs, but most of all, there are people. People can be the most dangerous of all. People can hurt you, ignore you, stab you in the back, front, from behind, all the while looking you straight in the eyes.

I worry mostly about other people and what harm they can do to my kids. Then I talk to myself like a crazy person. That's when I feel most crazy. When I think of how death is unannounced.

Listen to your own **voice** first.

What I learned from Prince

An intellect and a savoir-faire
Smart
Sexy
Compassionate
Peaceful
Creative
Intelligent
Poetic
Stylish
Love
Sex
Purple
Distance
Words
Music and Lyrics
A world of metaphors
River of blood
Sign of the times
Soul
Rhythm
Dance
Patience
Revolution
1999
my wedding song: 7
falling
breathing

independence
fighting the system
breaking rules
isolation
connection
controversy
head

Minnesota
Live shows
Talking sexy
Moans
Squeals
Naked
Driving
Red Corvette
Lovesexy
Feelings
Desire
Passion

Stay away from people who pull you down while you are drowning.

Misery loves company is an old adage that holds so much truth. There are people who bring out your darkness for their own joy. They want to talk about your past panic attacks or therapy sessions. They want you to feel as low as they are. They want you unhappy. I've seen it being done to me. Suddenly, my marriage is falling apart and my sex life is not good enough. Then I stop myself and say, 'wtf' am I saying?

Don't join a sinking ship. This is when you need to be a listener. Say nothing and float above the air.

I wake up a different person Every day Like the sunrise,

If you look
closely
It is never
identical.

Never mind what they told you to do.
Just
Do the opposite.

All I want to be is

a poem.

The rest is

unrealistic.

The Day
I feel no Poetry it
gets darker.

I only need a notebook and pen
to convert my tears
into words. They come
from the pink sky
at night and yellow
 sky
in the morning.

They whisper,
wake up
we are waiting for you.

I need to **write** to survive

I keep on changing
With the same face,
How odd it is to live so many lifetimes
In one.

I will always be a mystery even to myself

Freedom is being who you are
even when everyone thinks they know you
You keep surprising them
With your vulnerability.
I keep it intact and expose it
in selected poems.
I love to start over—
I thought it killed me
I drank too much, stopped writing
but I can never stop now.

Every day I am a different person.

It's not easy to feel the world on the tip of your fingers and not let it affect you

Being emotional is not really a choice. It's how some of us are made; it's in our DNA, in our blood, our history. Both my parents were criers; it was normal to see my dad crying. His eyes would get teary-eyed at most emotional events, as would my mom.

I try to hold back the tears, but when they come pouring down it's like a waterfall. I hate watching the news because that upsets me the most. Better to avoid it on a daily basis and live in my own world.

I am not of this century.

When I tweeted this, many people understood.

It feels as if my physical body is here in 2018,
but parts of me are stuck in another era—
circa
1499
1587
1691
1794
1896
1920
1973
I feel that time must have passed slower back
then
walking in gardens
working in fields
in times of famine
revolution
oppression
artistic expression
I hate checking my phone for messages
that are not there
instead of using up my time
with water and earth.

No matter
what happens
I never give
up
on the ones I
love...

I wrote this for my daughter, Maria, who struggled through the public and private school system and fell through the cracks. After so many different schools, different teachers, we found a school for her—an alternative school with a small classroom and ratio. If I had given up, she would have been a high school dropout…when it comes to our children we need to keep fighting for them, even after they have given up. We need to guide our kids, there is no one else looking out for them if the school system has let you down over and over. She graduated high school and is continuing school because of the constant search for what is best for her.

We need to sacrifice so much as parents and in the end, we don't know if our child will even succeed. In some situations, I have seen parents lose their mind over their kids; drug addiction, dropping out of school, and have ultimately abandoned them.

The main problem is that some parents abandon their children too soon. They give up so easily to continue living their lives and taking their trips.
I think if you stop guiding, no one will follow you.

As a parent, we can't ever stop giving advice and communicating.

If you have to second guess and be in the dark, you're worth better.

Stay beautiful and strong
When others try to break your soul,
It's not you
they want,
It's your beauty & art.

Relationships start with the first people who love you, The first who you loved back.

Not everyone grew up
in a loving home
with stable parents.
It's easy to give up
but it is so much
harder to keep going.
Getting up and taking
care of your kids,
your life, your job,
finding love. Nothing
is a formula. It's
Survival.

Say I love you.

Love a person for who they are not who you want them to be. Love yourself first. Stop hating your lover because of their faults. You need to either accept them or reject them. There is no perfect person out there for you; there is the one who never stops giving up on you, who is by your side through all the bullshit, the fights, the trauma. Life is light.

Poets want everything that you can't buy

Like nature
the universe
freedom
breaths of fresh air
words
poems
dancing with words
organic garden vegetables
time
love
a deep spiritual connection of soul mates.

Poets want to stay home and write, wearing the same shoes and forgetting to eat.

I need raw poetry in my veins

I love words as food. It fills up my appetite with parsley, mint, and spices. It has a way of keeping my immune system stronger—my senses alert, my feet tapping, and my soul smelling the aroma of imagery.

I fell in love with poetry because it loved me back more than anyone ever could.

The ocean heals scars seen and unseen

I was in Greece when I wrote this. When I go in the ocean the salt water cleanses all of my sins. It kisses my scars and caresses my pain. I have tendonitis. Only I know where it is— me and the ocean, our secret. She saves me by wrapping me up in her arms.

At least once a year I spend a week in the ocean. Twenty-minutes in the water each time you go in for a dip. If you live near the ocean, you are one of the lucky ones. Protect your skin though because too much of anything is never a good thing.

In Montreal, we are deprived of an ocean.

If writing hurts you're doing it right

Some writers believe this, others don't. I had so many trolls on this thought. So many who agree and others who disagree. However you feel about writing and whatever your state of mind, when I write about my own painful experiences in a poem, it hurts and I cry. Simple. I don't need therapy as much as I need poetry.

The act of hugging books instead of humans has cured me of loneliness

Right next to my bed, I have more books than anything else. I have poetry books, novels that I am reading—at least two at a time. My Anne Sexton, *Selected Poems*, keeps me company. I rely on my books to fall asleep. I rely on them in times when I need to escape reality. They have a way of hugging me. Words are comforting to me in a way that is hard to explain. My blue journal has gold letters, *Live the Story You Want to Tell.*

When I write in my journal and read it a few months later, it reminds me of the moments I had already forgotten about. When I read a great poem over and over again, it reminds me of how much I have to learn.

I think
in
parallel
universes

I write to
breathe.
Words are
My oxygen.

On Being Trilingual 3 phone calls

1.
9:00 a.m.
Me: Γεια σου, μαμά.
Πώς είσαι;
Mom: Μαγειρεύω φακές, δεν χρειάζεται να μαγειρεύεις.
Me: Αλλά, μαμά, δεν έχω φάει ούτε πρωινό!
Mom: Σας προετοιμάζω από τώρα.
Πρέπει να πάω στον κήπο για να κόψω φρέσκα βότανα.

Translation:
Me: Hi there, Mama.
how are you?
Mom: I'm cooking lentils, you don't have to cook.

Me: But, Ma, I haven't even eaten breakfast!
Mom: Well, I'm preparing you from now.
I have to go in the garden to cut fresh herbs.

She hangs up.

2.
9 :15
Operator : Ville de Laval, Comment puis-je vous aider?
Me : Bonjour, Qu'est-ce que je fais avec une batterie de voiture que je veux jeter?
Operator : Eh bien, vous pouvez voir si Canadien Tire le prend. Sinon, vous pouvez l'apporter à l'hôtel de ville le 15 septembre.
Me : Est-ce la seule fois que je peux l'apporter?
Operator : Oui, seulement trois fois par an.
Me : Quelle heure?
Operator : de 9h à 17h
Me : Je vous remercie
Operator : De rien
Me : Bonne journée.
Operator : Merci d'avoir appelé Ville de Laval.

Translation :
Operator: Ville de Laval, how can I help you?
Me: Hello, what do I do with a car battery that I want to throw out?
Operator: Well, you can see if Canadian Tire takes it. Otherwise, you can bring it to Hotel de Ville on Sept. 15th.
Me: Is that the only time I can bring it?
Operator: Yes, only three times a year.
Me: What time?
Operator: from 9-5 p.m.
Me: Thank you.
Operator: You're welcome.
Me: Have a good day.
Operator: Thank you for calling Ville de Laval.

3.
9:20
Greg: Did you make coffee?
Me: Yes, come in the kitchen.

I hear him walking from the bedroom.

Time to write and turn off the phone.

It's easy to tell a lie. It's the truth that has poets stumbling.

I'm having an affair with poetry

It is the lover I never had. It's the words I could never write. I wish I could write like Anne Sexton. I read her books and know that I can't write like that, but I admire it. I cherish her words like a lover staring at a photo of a loved one. I love reading Maya, Pablo, William—it's as if they are my secret lovers. I can dream inside their words and find a love that makes me smile to myself as if I have a secret.

Understand the poem, not the poet

In university, I learned to deconstruct; to take the poet out of the poem. When I read a poem, I dissect it from my own experience, not the poet. How do we know what is true or false? Fact or fiction? Fantasy and reality?

Take the poet out of the equation and connect with the words.

The poet is merely the messenger of your own experience.

I care more about what you're **not** telling me.

Sometimes you don't realize what is inside of you until it rages out and tackles you down.

I could be sitting and listening to the birds chirping on my summer vacation or be drinking my coffee or listening to music…when suddenly it comes at me like a tidal wave. I can't name it or believe it. It can be a belief or a lie. I can confuse both quite easily. I can fall for a lie—my eyes are somewhat closed. I feel the clouds and believe in them. I fear death yet welcome it. I want to hear I love you and say it many times a day. A good cry is needed. I need it badly. It comes out and makes me numb for a while. My world is quiet; it needs reflection.

If you think there is no more heartache inside of you, you are mistaken.

Isms

Heavenism
Hellism
Speedyism
Me-me-meism
Spunkyism
Greekism
Hystericalism
Boobyism
Skyism
Flowerism
Citizenism
Bakingism
Teachism
Poetism
Fuckism
Lovism
Twitterism
Chrissyism

If you can't poke fun at yourself what's the point?

If you enjoyed my book, please leave me a review on Amazon and Goodreads.
Thank you for reading this book.
Buy books, support writers.
Support the Arts.

About the Author

Christina Strigas is a writer, poet, and teacher. She works full-time as a public schoolteacher teaching French and English in Montreal, Quebec. Her poetry book *Love & Vodka* made "Your ultimate Canadian poetry list: 68 poetry collections recommended by you" by CBC News.

Social media links:
www.christinastrigas.com
Twitter: @christinastriga
Instagram: @c.strigas_sexyasspoet
Facebook: Christina Strigas Author

www.ingramcontent.com/pod-product-compliance
Lightning Source LLC
Chambersburg PA
CBHW030442010526
44118CB00011B/752